From *Below* to *Above*

From *Below* to *Above*

A young man's testimony of overcoming
homosexuality, drugs, and witchcraft

Shanahn Smith

Printed in the United States of America

Publishing services by Selah Publishing Group, LLC, Indiana. The views expressed or implied in this work do not necessarily reflect those of Selah Publishing Group.

ISBN: 1-58930-137-4
Library of Congress Control Number: 2004096831

Word of Christening

And I said, who are thou, Lord? And he said, I am Jesus whom thou persecutest.

But rise, and stand upon thy feet: for I have appeared unto thee for this purpose, to make thee a minister and a witness both of these things which thou hast seen, and of those things in the which I will appear unto thee;

Delivering thee from the people, and from the gentiles, unto whom now I send thee.

To open their eyes, and to turn them from darkness to light, and from the power of Satan unto God, that they may receive forgiveness of sins, and inheritance among them which are sanctified by faith that is in me.

Acts 26:15-18, KJV

Dedicated in loving memory to all the lives lost to HIV/AIDS, drug addiction and suicide.

Acknowledgements

I would like to thank my mother and family for supporting me, even when they couldn't understand me and for always loving me even during my times of confusion.

To Rebecca Conn and Pastor Kari Ifland who took the time to share their knowledge and wisdom for the revisions of this book. The extra time and patience you've shown me will always be remembered in the pages of this book.

To my Lord and Savior Jesus Christ, thank You for loving our Father enough to complete His work regardless of the pain and humiliation You knew You would have to endure. Mere words will never express the gratitude I feel for Your act or express the sorrow I feel that my sinful life inflicted You with so much.

To my Father in Heaven, I give you worship and praise. Without You I would have never found my Lord and Savior, nor would I have gained the happiness and unmovable joy that comes only from knowing You. May You reign forever and always upon my mind, body, and soul and May Your personal will always be fulfilled upon this earth.

Contents

Foreword 13

From Below to Above 15

Prayers to the Heavenly Father 36-41

Q & A with the Author 55

Supporting Bible Scriptures
   i. Sexual Immorality 65
   ii. Substance Abuse and Drug Addictions . . 73
   iii. Witchcraft 76
   ix. Obscene Language and Crude Joking . . . 88

Since the completion of this book 91
   (an update on the author)

Foreword

Life is a journey. How often have you read that statement? In this confused and broken world, I would venture to say that many are coming ever closer to this truth. No matter your interest in religion or spiritual issues, indeed we are spiritual beings on a spiritual quest towards completeness and wholeness in our lives.

There is a tidal wave of spiritual guides, cult leaders, gurus, and motivators, all leading in different ways – each claiming to possess the directions for life's spiritual journey. Are you a part of the traveling mass that has become confused, disoriented, and probably completely lost? Or maybe life as you know it is a shipwreck of failures, wrong choices, addictions, abuse, neglect, anger and destruction. "From Below to Above" may very well be the course chart for a new beginning. Need direction? Need to be set free? Need tears wiped away? Need Hope? Shanahn Smith's journey, back from hell itself, is for you.

Be blessed and strengthened on your journey, "From Below to Above."

Pastor George Lee Glass
Grace Church
DeRidder Louisiana

From Below to Above

My name is Shanahn Smith -pronounced Shannon, for those of you confused with the spelling. At the time of the writing of this book, I'm a twenty-four year old male with an eighth grade education having grown up in a small town in northwest Georgia. "The First Mountain City" is bannered across each water tower and most of the city signs. It is a small town screaming for advancement, but in the same breath holding on to old values.

I live on my mother's eighty-eight acre farm with her, my older sister and my niece. Quaint, you might think? Sometimes! We've all been through our own journeys, giving each one of us experiences suitable for a great book. Especially my mother! Having raised five children and living through several abusive marriages, she could tell you some horror stories. However, she got by one day at a time, each day attempting to walk closer with our Lord and Savior.

This book is the true story of my life—a life that was filled with homosexuality, drugs and witchcraft, perversion and debauchery, multiple suicide attempts and drug overdoses. This is not a book attempting to make light of my mistakes or to glorify sin; it is rather, a chance, I hope, to reach thousands in similar situations. This book is a tool to help people break free from the bondage of sin and destroy the shackles of control the enemy has upon their life.

> **Jesus replied, "I tell you the truth, everyone who sins is a slave to sin."**
> JOHN 8:34

In the pages of this book, I hope to bring you to a place of repentance and wisdom concerning your life in relation to what the Bible says. I urge you to follow along with me in your Bible, not taking my word for it, but looking for yourself into the Word of the Lord. Make your own decisions based on what you read as you read it. It's not the words or opinions of others that will save you, but the opinion of the Lord, which he will plant in you and cause to grow as you read the Bible and pray.

Since you've taken the time to purchase this book, you probably already sense a lack of fulfillment in your life, and to some degree have the knowledge of right from wrong. If you've received this book as a gift and have been able to read this far, quickly ask yourself why this book has come to you. Could it be that the Lord has put it in your life out of love for you? It's a good possibility. So I urge you to keep reading, if for no other reason than to see how my previous lifestyle nearly destroyed all chances of any fulfillment. What do you have to lose? Except maybe some pain…

As a minister, it would be easy to come out of the gate immediately gay bashing and throwing Bible bullets, telling you how wrong it is and how you're going to go to Hell if you are gay. However, what good would that do? I know from experience that you, if you are struggling with homosexuality, already have enough coming against you. From the constant rejection by friends, family and loved ones to the Bible-beaters who stand among you proclaiming your damnation, the last thing you need from this book is one more reason to make you feel isolated and rejected. By now, you've probably perfected that feeling. What I want to do is let you know that you are not alone and that I'm with you. Even better yet, the Lord our Savior is with you now and forever. Welcome to the journey that will lead you closer to Him and His ways.

My feelings of confusion started around twelve years of age. I was a loving child who stood out due to my manners and proper respect for my elders, which my mother had properly screamed into me, God love her. Slowly, I became an outcast, enhanced by my actions towards other males. What started out as a harmless desire to want to be more like them, turned into something far worse in the end. The words "I wish" still ring in my ears today. My mind would race with thoughts like, "I wish I acted more like him. I wish I looked more like him. I wish I was him." Finally, in time, those thoughts turned into, "I wish I was anyone other than myself."

The harder I tried to fit in, the more I was rejected. I became more confused regarding my emotions and feelings. As the years passed and my hormones kicked in, the "I wish I looked and acted like him" became somewhat sexual and then slowly became, "I wish I could be with him."

My personal desire to be anyone other than myself had taken over my mind. It was what I constantly dreamed and breathed. My imagination was running rampant in daydreams of how much happier I would be if I were "him" —whoever "he" represented that day— never seeing that other people or "he" had problems, too. It became such an obsession that when my mind began to realize that I couldn't be them, I began to think I could still be with them sexually. These thoughts gave the devil one more way to lead me away into sin.

Please understand that regardless of your personal beliefs in Heaven and Hell, good and evil, Satan and the Lord God Almighty—they are very real. Every day our lives are a constant spiritual battle—even when we don't see it or recognize it.

Because of how bad I considered my life to be and because I was tormented daily, I quickly turned the blame on God and became consumed with dislike and hatred for anyone and anything speaking on His behalf. At first, I hated Him for allowing such pain and rejection to happen to me. Then, I hated Him for making me different. Then, I hated Him for making me gay. Then, I hated Him, most of all, for not answering any of my prayers, especially those in which I cried myself to sleep each night, asking Him to end my life.

I was hurting and I felt rejected, even from the Lord. I felt like a mistake - an ugly, horrible mistake who had been forsaken and then forgotten. In my mind I felt absolutely and totally isolated—having no one to turn to or be comforted by.

My days became a constant reminder of what seemed like a never-ending curse. Day after day, new battles raged on. Severe wounds were inflicted, many times pushing me to the point of emotional death. And with each and every wound came an additional scar. Each scar represented a new wall being built—walls that for so long towered above me, looming over me like the night sky to a lost sailor. But, just as there are stars in the heaven, so there is light in the darkness.

Throughout my middle school years, I dealt with much rejection. My family scrambled to seek teachers, counselors, doctors and principles to help. Unfortunately, most were unable, or were unwilling, to help. My deteriorating condition was something that was overlooked in hopes that it would go away. It's a constant reminder of how small-town politics work and how ineffective a school system is without the Lord present. However, that's a different book altogether.

Rejection and sexual confusion slowly destroyed my childhood and my life. I spent more time alone and isolated. Lunchtime became a battlefield and break time an all out war. It didn't take long for me to understand my best interest was to hide out. I quickly took up refuge from the war in an empty band room where I spent each day without food or friends. Now, as bad as it might sound, I'm sure there are others who have similar stories or still others with even worse stories than mine.

I became accustomed to the isolation. If you don't know of anything else, how can you expect to hope for anything else? Right? Well, years slowly ticked by—each year getting worse. Physical violence became an issue and so did my grades. More importantly, though, was my health. Due to depression and loss of appetite, my lack of growth became a concern, which brought on further despair and anxiety.

Finally, in my eighth grade year, I was pulled from the school system—only after I spent half of the year in the counselor's office. I attempted to convince her of anything that would help me to escape, eventually blaming my desire to leave public school and enter into home school, on my mother's personal safety. It was a true concern—a valid issue, but not the real problem. Not only was I having problems in school, but my home life was also out of whack.

My father, attempting to do his best, often worked long hours. The extra time at work only led to added pressures which left him very disconnected from the family and irritable. His anger would ultimately turn toward my mother as he preached how everything was wrong, placing a large portion of the blame on her. My mother was no saint, but my father was no hero.

Before you start blaming everything on the absence of a father figure, or maybe even family violence, let me say that I don't blame my father or my mother, nor do I believe that in all cases these are the reasons for homosexuality. I know that for me it wasn't the cause, but it surely wasn't the cure. I don't want you to think I hold anger towards my father - I forgave him long before he ever left. I understand your situation might be different, but I urge you now to let it go. Forgiving your parents will most definitely be your first step. Forgiving yourself will without a doubt be your last step.

Shortly after being pulled from school, I came to realize what once was my safe haven had now become my prison. The very walls that protected me from the world held me hostage from a life. Due to overwhelming anxiety, it became impossible for me to leave the house or the farm. My parents would beg me to go to town with them. However, each time I did, it quickly became an incident. For nearly a year, I had very little to do with the outside world.

My depression grew and saturated my body and mind, distorting reality. My need to find reasoning behind my rejection from the world became an obsession—eventually leading me to blame everything on my personal appearance.

I remember looking in the mirror and being consumed with hatred and disgust. Gazing at all the flaws and mistakes, I found myself thinking, "No wonder everyone hates me - look at how ugly I am." In the end, this behavior built the stronghold I still struggle with today - "It's all because of the way I look!"

As this obsession with my looks grew, so did my depression and thoughts of suicide. It got so bad that, for a time, I was unable even to look into a mirror. I recall that the experience of getting a haircut was a nightmare. To sit in front of the mirror looking at myself, while others watched, was pure agony. It had such a negative effect that I would sleep most of the day away to forget the image.

I had finally come to the point of being a danger to myself. However, I no longer possessed the energy to get out of bed, much less load a gun and pull the trigger. Yet, that time did come...

Many of you may have faced similar experiences when it comes to growing up gay. To the ones who haven't, I can only say I would never wish this lifestyle of confusion on anyone. It's not a lifestyle at all. It's a death sentence to not only our emotions, but also our souls. It produces feelings and emotions that sometimes are far worse than the mere same-sex attraction. Rage, hostility, despair, delusion, perversion and homicidal tendencies are just some of the repercussions of feeling emotionally abandoned and rejected from society and God's love.

Homosexuality becomes a lifestyle of sexual indulgence and perversion. You seek happiness and love, willing to do whatever it takes to find someone to love you. In the end, you accept and justify the terms of such moral degradation for a chance to be happy. The very thing that for so long I cursed and hated became the very thing I ended up speaking out for and holding firm to—protecting my "gay rights" in every breath.

Religion has become a controversial topic in the gay community. Preachers, pastors, ministers and teachers of the faith are viewed as the enemy, leaving the gay community to search for "once again" someone to accept them and love them for who they are. The result is the creation of a movement in false religions and beliefs that are founded on doctored theories and opinions of the Bible that make it acceptable to "practice" homosexuality and lesbianism.

There are other people, like myself at one point, who out of defense and ignorance of the Bible say things like:

- "No where in the Bible does it say I'm going to hell for being gay"
- "I was born gay. Are you saying that God made a mistake?"
- "It might be a sin, but a sin is a sin. Who are you to judge me? Is that not a sin in it self?"
- "Why would God punish me for just seeking love, or wanting to find love?"
- "How could God allow me to be this way if he didn't approve?"

- "If it was as easy as pushing a button, don't you think I would've pushed it along time ago? How can you think I choose this? I can't be anything different than this."

I used each and every one of these excuses over the years, not once ever picking up a Bible, knowing nothing concerning God. However, I managed not only to convince others, but also to gather a following of supporters. I successfully changed their minds and caused people to accept and understand more and more of my way of thinking. I became a gay rights activist speaking out for my rights and living an active and open gay lifestyle. I traveled throughout the states and the Keys to attend Gay Pride events—a festival of homosexuals, lesbians, and their rights—leaving a trail of sexual encounters and experiences everywhere I went. I hid nothing from family, friends or the outside world. I even helped others in the same situation, young and old, in dealing with and accepting their emotions.

Today I look back and I see my mistakes with a heavy heart. Attempting to help others like myself, I only added to their confusion. It was a mistake that I deeply regret. As far as being a gay man or woman, do I feel or think you have rights? "Yes!" - Without doubt—without question—without fear! As a human being you have a right to live without physical or mental attacks from others. But as a child of God, you have the right to be free from the confusion, pain, and suffering that the gay lifestyle will cause you. As a child of God and a believer in Christ, you can have the ability to live a life of fulfillment. You can live a life that will possess the love you long for— the love of a man who will protect you from this world of sin and rejection. It's a love so strong that no drug or fleshly pleasure can ever match what He has promised and desires to send to you. All you have to do is ask.

> **Yet to all who received him, to those who believed in his name, he gave the right to become children of God – Children born not of natural descent, nor of human decision or a husband's will, but born of God.**
> JOHN 1:12

> **For sin shall not be your master, because you are not under law, but under Grace.**
> ROMANS 6:14

> **You have been set free from sin and have become slaves to righteousness.**
> ROMANS 6:18

> **Therefore do not let sin reign in your mortal body so that you obey its evil desires. Do not offer the parts of your body to sin, as instruments of wickedness, but rather offer yourselves to God, as those who have been brought from death to life; and offer the parts of your body to him as instruments of righteousness.**
> ROMANS 6:12-13

By my early teens my life had become a pit of despair with my only escape found during sleep. The days slipped by as my body slipped into a coma-like state, waiting for death. All hope was lost and so was my will to live. As my condition deteriorated, my parents sensed a new urgency to seek help for me. New doctors and physicians entered my life, each with a different opinion and various medications to treat my condition. The introduction of medications was a good start but a dangerous risk to a truly depressed person. Because of the effects of the medication, I no longer had the ability to sleep all day, which my family saw as an improvement. Instead, the results gave me more of an awareness of how much I wanted to die backed now with the energy to do something about it.

So it began. Entertaining the idea of suicide became a plan in the making—a debate within myself of what I was willing to do and not do. My house was filled with multiple avenues of self-termination. Handguns and rifles littered my home. However, each time I attempted to use one, I could never get my body to obey. Several times I had a gun up in my face, mouth, and against my temple. However, my trembling finger could never function correctly. Thank the Lord! After many attempts, I put the option of suicide behind me, experiencing additional depression from my inability even to kill myself. This began what would be a nearly ten-year obsession of drug addiction and overdoses.

Around fourteen I made my first attempt at an overdose. I gathered together all of my depression medication, sleeping pills and aspirin that I could find and, with little fear, swallowed what I thought would be an end to my misery. Needless to say, it didn't work. My father arrived home, unaware of my suicide attempt, and asked me to take a drive with him. After his continual refusal to take no for an answer, I finally gave in. At some point during our drive I passed out. I awakened the next day in my bed. My parents assumed I had caught a cold so my mother took care of me, nursing me back to health—never knowing my true condition.

Imagine feeling like a failure and constantly failing even at your suicide attempts. It finally sent me over the deep end and back to my bed where I slept more than ever. Then, one day, a young male from my neighborhood showed up with his friend from school. For some unknown reason they wanted me to go ride around with them. At the time, I was so shocked that I didn't give it much thought. My parents were even confused. Where did they come from? Why did they show up so unexpectedly, especially showing an interest in being my friends?

My newfound friends quickly led me astray and deeper into sin. I found the joy of disobedience and the pleasure of rebellion. Coming from a mother who sheltered and protected me, I did have many struggles, and the devil had many ways of comforting me and leading me further into darkness. What began with foul language turned into smoking, drinking, and ultimately drugs and even an addiction to masturbation. With each new step, it grew easier to push past my morals and ethics. Each step appeared to lead me away from that voice of conviction, what some of us call our conscience, but what the Bible teaches is the Holy Spirit.

> **And I will ask the Father, and he will give you another Counselor to be with you forever- the Spirit of Truth. The world cannot accept him, because it neither sees him nor knows him. But you know him, for he lives with you and will be in you.**
> JOHN 14:16-17

Because of my need for acceptance from my friends and the world, my ability to say "no" to anything diminished quickly to nothing. Their acceptance became a driving force from which I pulled strength. I would attempt things my friends would not, holding nothing back. I had no sense of when to stop.

The years passed and so did my relationships with old friends. As I moved through the chain of drugs and friends, my sexual desires increased as well as my need for companionship. The number of attempts to find someone skyrocketed. I had several experiences with different male friends, many of whom are straight and married today. This experience shows me that young males frequently experiment with sexuality while trying to figure out who they are. During the same time, I also saw firsthand the mistakes you can make when your judgment is altered by substances.

My ladder of drug addiction went as followed:
1. Marijuana
2. Acid (LSD)
3. Bathtub crank (speed)
4. Cocaine
5. Ecstasy
6. Heroin
7. Crack cocaine
8. Special K (cat tranquilizers)
9. GHB (date-rape drug)
10. ICE (crystal methamphetamines)

I started using needles a little before I took part in heroin for the first time. I hated heroin but became a prisoner to shooting up cocaine or crack cocaine. Shooting up put me on my deathbed several times, scaring my friends and family on more than one occasion. One such occasion was on Thanksgiving Day. After sneaking away from the family, I hid away in my room so I could shoot up. I must have misjudged the dose because the next thing I knew I was convulsing and seizing as severe pain shot through my body. It brought me so close to death that it truly terrified me for a moment, yet that fear and pain were no match for my personal destructive attitude and desire to die. After fifteen minutes, I was busy fixing the now dull syringe, and continued throughout the night to attempt to get the same effect.

Oh how freedom rings in our ears as we head out into the world for the first time, released from the confines of our parents and their rules. We race into the world convinced of our maturity, intelligence and our parent's lack thereof. We believe ourselves to be indestructible and often incorruptible. We long for freedom and responsibility. We seek acceptance and understanding. But we end up with mistakes and their repercussions. Freedom is no longer what we once thought, but becomes death and destruction. Ultimately we stand shackled to the world, in bondage to the enemy, just as I was in bondage to drugs.

> **Do not love the world or anything in the world. If anyone loves the world, the love of the father is not in him. For everything in the world –the cravings of sinful man, the lust of the eyes and the boasting of what he has and does- comes not from the father but from the world. The world and its desires pass away, but the man who does the will of God lives forever.**
> 1ˢᵗ JOHN 2:15-17

> **You, dear children, are from God, and have overcome them, because the one who is in you is greater than the one who is in the world.**
> 1ˢᵗ JOHN 4:4

For everyone born of God overcomes the World.

1st JOHN 5:4, EMPHASIS ADDED

For God so loved the world that he gave his one and only son, that whoever believes in him shall not perish but have eternal life. For God did not send his Son into the world to condemn the world, but to save the world through him. Whoever believes in him is not condemned, but whoever does not believe stands condemned already because he has not believed in the name of God's one and only Son.

JOHN 3:16-18

The world is full of sin and detestable things. Our hearts and minds are hardened and calloused concerning worldly issues. Things that at one time would bother us simply have little or no effect on us anymore. Things we would never consider doing in the past suddenly don't seem to be as big an issue as before. Why is this so? The answer is Lucifer, also known as Satan. He is of this world and stands condemned along with all who follow in his ways. His followers become his children— destined to share eternity with their father, an eternity far worse than anything we can imagine or even comprehend. Nothing we have ever heard, seen or felt in this world will compare to the torment he and his followers will endure forever. It will be an eternity of pain and hurt greater than what any of us have lived through or are going through today.

Fortunately, God so loved the world and you and me that He sent His one and only Son to die for our sins. He sacrificed the very thing that made the world, the heavens, the stars and the sky for our ability to be forgiven and reconciled with Him. Our Father, the Creator and our God, gave His "Word" in the form of a Son. He came to earth as a man, made to hang from a tree and become everything that He wasn't. From righteousness, perfection and truth to lawlessness, sin and lies - no greater love has there ever been, and no greater love will there ever be.

In His act of love toward us, He has given us the ability to walk from our sins and darkness into righteousness and light.

> **Therefore, there is now no condemnation for those who are in Christ Jesus, because through Christ Jesus the law of the spirit of life set me free from the law of sin and death.**
> ROMANS 8:1-2

> **Therefore, if anyone is in Christ, he is a new creation; the old has gone, the new has come!**
> 2nd CORINTHIANS 5:17

As the influence of drugs and friends continued, I found myself further down the road of destruction. Just about every night I could be found hanging out in the nightclubs of Atlanta, frequenting gay bars, which offered connections to others like myself. The atmosphere was a breeding ground for new addictions, drugs, sexual sins and perversion. I watched the lifestyle swallow up young newcomers and leave them confused, hurting and alone. (Worse, some were confused, hurting, alone and now infected with HIV and/or Hepatitis.) I can recall the names and faces of my friends—young males like myself—who are now HIV positive. There were many of them with whom I had spent personal and intimate time. I know in my heart I should be sick, along with them. I've been saved only by the grace of God, which has humbled me now to the point of tears. I remember one guy who received the virus before he was eighteen. Another found out that he was infected after receiving a letter from his boyfriend. The boyfriend left with everything my friend owned, leaving only a letter warning, "Get tested!" Another was in his early twenties. I had only spent a limited amount of time with him—a time cut short as a result of his suicide. His body was found in his home—alone—with a gun at his side. (I pray God may grant peace to his soul).

This confusion that we label a "lifestyle" is not a lifestyle. It's an acceptance and submission to our own deaths. You might argue with me or think differently. You might even try to justify it. I did! The truth is that each day spent living in this confusion and accepting it as a way of life is another day you move closer to spiritual death and to a place of no return.

The older and more experienced one becomes in the gay lifestyle, the more aware one becomes of its lack of fulfillment. That hope of finding someone to have a relationship with becomes a thing of the past. The dream of finding that attractive man that will love you and be faithful becomes a joke. Anger and bitterness become one's only companions and friends. Unfortunately, by this time, many feel trapped with no way out.

Don't travel down the same road of destruction that I did. Don't lose or forfeit your right to happiness as I did. My life was filled with worldly pleasures, fulfilling to the flesh... but then what? After the high is gone and you're coming down, what has been achieved? After the sexual pleasure and the orgasms are over, who's left? What long-term happiness do you have to carry you through your life? Or, more importantly, what do you face at the end of the day if today is your last day? What would eternity be like for you? Would it be filled with love or disaster, comfort or greater pain than life has ever shown you?

Because of my hatred and confusion towards God, I had chosen to turn away from any religious organizations. I even went as far as to speak against all of them. I found my comfort in pagan rituals, calling myself a witch, and maintaining a powerful dedication to a pagan way of thinking. I spent many years of my life gathering various pagan tools, oils, books and idols. I wandered in and out of white magic, black magic and voodoo. On several occasions, I spent time with open, active Satanists and demon worshipers. (I even traveled to Savannah on several occasions to stock up on supplies, meeting with a fellow member of the pagan faith—a black magic witch.)

I never once realized what I was doing or what the Bible said about witchcraft. I didn't even realize the Bible spoke on and against pagan practices. It was never discussed in any of the witchcraft books I had read. The one thing the books do teach is that in witchcraft there is no satanic influence, or at least most don't embrace it. They teach that only one god exists—no devil. Their god produces both good and evil for the greater good. Their god is not a man or a woman but both—the god of the sun and the goddess of the night. This concept becomes a snare for anyone seeking acceptance and power without fear of punishment.

As I grew in the art of witchcraft, I experienced demonic spirits on several occasions. Although I reaped the consequences of my beliefs, I now stand free from their influence. With this freedom, today I realize that the deeper I went into darkness, the worse I became. In time, God gave me over to Satan, allowing the sin to run its course as an act of judgment. As a result, I lost what little self-control I had left and found myself captive to things like prostitution and other sexual acts I would have never thought of doing before. My self-respect became a thing of the past as my mind became a holding cell for demons and evil spirits.

Along with the loss of self-control, I also began to hear voices and see evil spirits at night. They taunted and attacked me during my sleep. Sometimes I would be awakened out of my sleep with the feeling that I was being sexually attacked—finding myself with a nocturnal emission—my skin still crawling and stinging. Confused and scared, I would blame anything, including past drug use. I was giving way to the thoughts that I was losing my mind. I never once considered that my spiritual beliefs or the large altar that I had erected in my room could have had anything to do with it. I couldn't understand at the time that I was possessed with an Antichrist spirit. I actively promoted the very one who was trying to destroy me, embracing the very evil that was raping my mind and body.

Pagan beliefs have infiltrated the gay lifestyle. Not all the beliefs come with the label of witchcraft or Satanism. More commonly, you find the title "New Age Beliefs." But regardless of the name, the act is still the same. It is a rejection of the true God for that which is a mimic and very much demonic. You find that people of all ages seeking acceptance and understanding start seeking power and control as a result of feeling rejected. In their search for love, I've witnessed many gay men turn to burning candles and chanting rhymes or spells, never understanding the harm it could bring. Of course, not everyone who burns candles or chants does so with malice in their hearts. Unfortunately, ever so slowly, they are corrupted by the very power they embrace, never fully comprehending the evil they've tapped into. The process is so slow that they, in no way, notice it gradually changing their life and their actions.

My belief in witchcraft started out exactly the same way it does for a lot of gay men. A lonely heart, a simple prayer (also known as a spell), a small candle, and place to burn it – all backed by years of hurt, rejection and desperation. Within two short years I had dedicated a large wall and entertainment cabinet in my room to pagan beliefs. Along with the new collection of wiccan and fantasy paraphernalia, my interest and desires were suddenly catapulted forward into the arena of science fiction. Anything that presented an escape from reality, I believed and ultimately put my faith in. During this period of time, the manifestation of demonic forces began to appear in my room and my life. These demonic forces were also visible to my friends on occasion. During that period of two years, demonic attacks came against me mentally, physically and sexually.

Take this as a clear warning - Don't play around with something that you don't understand. Understand that words have power. Don't be like many who say, "I'm a pagan," or, "I'm a white or good witch," and never know what it means to be either of them or more importantly who they actually represent. Just the verbal confession gives Lucifer and his evil spirits an open door into your life. I caution you, don't simply become a child of Satan because you seek acceptance from this world. Don't think because you're gay or confused that you need the help of a candle to find love. Realize that just because you don't see the evidence of your pagan or new age beliefs doesn't mean that you haven't already been blinded by them. A truly deceived person will never know he is deceived. Just because you haven't seen demons and unclean spirits, doesn't mean they are not currently working in your life.

Today the Lord waits for you—longing to see you happy, fulfilled and no longer consumed with fear, doubt and confusion. Never again do you have to feel alone with tear-stained cheeks, harassed by suicidal thoughts. Today the Lord wants to see you come to know Him and His Father. He desires to cleanse you of your mistakes and set you free from your sins. He is longing to restore you as His child as He prepares you for your destiny— the destiny the devil has been attempting to make you forfeit since birth.

Now that you're aware of my past and my mistakes, you might say you've done worse, or you might think you could never live so horribly. Regardless of what you have or haven't done, the point is that Christ Jesus died for all our sins. While we were still sinners, He laid his life down for us—a true act of love.

Here is a trustworthy saying that deserves full acceptance: Christ Jesus came into the world to save sinners- of whom I am the

worst. But for that very reason I was shown mercy so that in me, the worst of sinners, Christ Jesus might display his unlimited patience as an example for those who would believe on him and receive eternal life.
1st Timothy 1:15-16

"Neither this man nor his parents sinned," said Jesus, "but this happened so that the work of God might be displayed in his life."
John 9:3

Today I ask you to pray a simple prayer with me before we continue. Through salvation, Christ will give you strength and wisdom from His Word. With the help of His Holy Spirit, you will break free of Satan and the bondages of sin he has placed on your life.

For we know that our old self was crucified with him so that the body of sin might be done away with, that we should no longer be slaves to sin – because anyone who has died has been freed from sin.
Romans 6:6-7

Prayer of Salvation

Father God,
Today I come before you a sinner, a sinner who for too long has made no effort to know you or your Son. I would like to apologize and ask for your forgiveness. Please, Heavenly Father, forgive me of all of my sins by the power of Your Son's precious blood. I believe that your Son Jesus Christ came to earth from a virgin birth, was beaten and then crucified on the cross for the for-

giveness of my sins and three days later, by Your divine power, rose again from the grave. Today, Father God, I ask to know Jesus Christ as my Lord and Savior and you as my Heavenly Father.

In Christ Jesus Name,
Amen

Homosexuality

Father God, Lord Jesus...

I call out today to the heavens, longing for your presence in my life. I confess any and all of my sins, admitting to each and every one. I blame no one for my mistakes and today accept complete responsibility for all of my actions. I cry out in my confusion concerning my sexuality, understanding that these feelings are wrong and lead to unhappiness, lack of fulfillment and separation from You. I ask for this confusion to now be removed and for my life and soul to be set free from this lust and unnatural desire.

Today, Lord, I ask you to reveal the devil's lies and unmask his presence in my life and mind. Set me free from this long-standing bondage.

In Your name Lord I pray - in the name of Jesus.
Amen

Drugs, Alcohol, Cigarettes

Father God, Lord Jesus,

I come before your throne a sinner, shackled by my weaknesses. I confess my sins of addiction now to you and accept responsibility for each one. I understand that my body is a temple of the Holy Spirit—a temple that I've desecrated with drugs, nicotine and alcohol. I ask for forgiveness for these offenses I've committed against my body and the Holy Spirit. I ask now to be released from the control of these addictions and the evil spirits that go along with them. I pray for new strength and power over my flesh and my desires. I ask also for the healing power of Christ to fall upon me. I ask Jesus to heal the damage I've done to my mind and my body.

Today Lord I offer my mind, body and soul to you. I ask with a heavy heart for the return of your love into my life. I welcome you now with the understanding and desire that my life will never be the same. Fill me Lord with your presence and remove all my worldly desires. Make me a true servant of the Lord.

In the name of Jesus I pray. Amen.

Witchcraft

Father God,
I come before you ashamed and disgusted for my ignorance. I admit and confess my horrific sins against you, your Son, the Holy Spirit, and the Living Word. I know this act against you is far worse than any other. Today I have felt your presence in my life and my heart.

I know that today my life can't stay the same. I lay down my mind, body, and soul before you. With remorse in my heart and distaste in my mouth for my actions, I ask forgiveness for these sins in the name of Jesus. I renounce any and all connections with familiar spirits, spirit guides, demons, or other pagan beliefs. I renounce any and all involvement with Wicca magic, spell casting, candle burning, horoscopes, tarot cards, psychics and other satanic tools. I renounce any and all sexual spirits and ask forgiveness for being involved in such a dark, demonic, satanic practices. Lord Jesus, I ask now to be cleansed from my past life and to be set free from Satan and all his evil. I ask you to remove all confusion from my mind, heart and soul. I ask you to cleanse me and apply your blood to my life and soul. Bring me Lord Jesus to know you and my Father's ways.

In the name of Jesus I pray. Amen

If you've prayed those prayers with me from a sincere heart, then your prayers have been answered and your forgiveness has been granted. Your name is now written in the Book of Life—your Salvation confirmed. However, I don't want you to stop there. I want you to say one more prayer with me. This prayer will be for the baptism of the Holy Spirit, which will help you to overcome this world.

> **Do not leave Jerusalem, but wait for the gift my Father promised, which you have heard me speak about. For John baptized with water, but in a few days you will be baptized with the Holy Spirit.**
> ACTS 1:4-5

> **But you will receive power when the Holy Spirit comes on you; and you will be my witnesses in Jerusalem, and in all Judea and Samaria, and to the ends of the earth.**
> ACTS 1:8

> **When the apostles in Jerusalem heard that Samaria had accepted the word of God, they sent Peter and John to them. When they arrived, they prayed for them that they might receive the Holy Spirit, because the Holy Spirit had not yet come upon any of them; they had simply been baptized into the**

name of the Lord Jesus. Then Peter and John placed their hands on them, and they received the Holy Spirit.

ACTS 8:14-17

When Paul placed his hands on them, the Holy Spirit came on them, and they spoke in tongues and prophesied. There were about twelve men in all.

ACTS 19:6-7

Prayer for Baptism of the Holy Spirit

Father God, Lord Jesus-

I call out to you in great love and respect. I thank you for forgiving me of my sins and saving my life. I thank you for setting me free from this world and the sin I found myself in. You are truly an awesome God and Savior. Using this book and these words as a point of contact—right now I raise my hands to you in praise and prayer, asking now for the Holy Spirit to wash over me and through me, leaving me with the ability to take on the world and Satan. I pray you plant a seed of faith and zeal in me to read the Bible and a desire and need to help others like myself.

May I now receive and know my Counselor.

In the mighty name of Jesus I pray. Amen.

Congratulations! I know without doubt or fear that if you have prayed those prayers with a truly sincere heart a smile is now forming across your face with a sudden feeling of happiness and release now welling up from inside of you.

Welcome to the Love of the Lord....

Father God, I come into agreement right now with each and every soul praying these prayers. I pray for your strength, love and grace to fall from the heavens upon each one of them. I pray and ask for my words to be a point of contact and that right now each individual would receive the Baptism of the Holy Spirit, submerging them totally and filling them completely, leaving every one of them a new person in Christ Jesus.

In the name of Jesus I pray.

Amen.

Shanahn C. Smith

By now you might wonder how I came to know the love of my Heavenly Father. What was it that caused me to change from my life of sin and destruction to a life of devotion and love? Are you ready to hear the unheard? I pray your mind and heart will feel the truth behind my words and allow you the ability to believe and have faith and trust in the power of God and our Lord and Savior Jesus Christ.

> **The fear of the Lord leads to life, and he who has it will abide in satisfaction; He will not be visited with evil.**
> PROVERBS 19:23, NKJV

On February 2, 2003, after a three-day binge of shooting up crystal methamphetamines, my body was weak, dehydrated, and deprived of food. I had reached my body's limit and the end of the Lord's patience. That night as I lay in my bed hurting, longing for sleep but unable to achieve it, I felt my body, down deep, begin to slowly slip away. At first I didn't understand what was happening.

I thought I was just really tired and really high from the speed. Quickly it became clear that my life was in danger. Suddenly, my mind, which was far from being sober, became clear. This sudden change both confused and alarmed me. I lay there hurting and puzzled. Noises began to roll from down in my bowels - a horrible sound of moaning accompanied by pain in my back and kidneys. Unable to decide what was taking place, I decided to simply wait and see if I would be okay.

Within minutes beings appeared, standing at the end of my bed. First there was only one, then others followed. Shadows with the appearance and characteristic of human beings lingered in the room. With each passing moment they became more coherent. I began to hear their calls to each other and to me. I could hear their voices carrying on conversations and sneering. They began to speak to me, telling me they were angels sent from heaven. However, my heart told me differently. I watched as they became more aware of me, and I became more aware of them. It appeared that they entered from the wall where the wiccan alter and pentagram stood. Some of them were distorted and disfigured. Both male and females were present. I watched as the males masturbated, performing sexual acts with each other.

Then a sudden movement from near my closed bedroom door grabbed my attention. I watched as a large demonic force entered into my room. Immediately there became a presence of pure evil—one that made my skin crawl and my mind swim. It was a presence of death—a power that notably made the others pull back. I realized the authority and power of this being was far greater from the reactions of the others, but also from its form and shape. Unlike the others, it towered above me, disfigured and burnt. It was expressionless and showing no signs of comprehension or reason, only subjection and obedience to some darker power. As it stood staring and swaying, I noticed its hands were actively doing something, as if conjuring or calling.

Just then I heard a voice that came bringing hope, but also paralyzing fear. I looked in the opposite direction, as if I somehow knew help stood waiting. I saw a shimmer of light and then heard a voice different from the others. A stern voice spoke with authority as I was told to move quickly out of the room. Then a flash of revelation ran through my mind. It became clear to me that the intent of the demon was to collect my soul and bring an end to my life. At first I was almost unable to move. Quickly, however, I broke free of the fear as I felt my life slipping away and a new light- headedness overtaking me. I stumbled out of the room and down the hall, and fell into my mother's empty bedroom. I called out with tears and a voice of panic: "Oh, help me Lord! What have I done?"

At that very moment, I heard a man's voice whisper, "JOHN 3:16." Not understanding what it meant, I cried out once again for help, and once again the voice said, "JOHN 3:16." Because of my ignorance concerning the Bible, I had no idea what it meant. I looked down the hall and could see the evil spirits and the demon lingering in my room slowly creeping forward.

I began to panic, and fear overtook my body as I screamed one last time, "OH GOD, I'M SORRY. PLEASE HELP ME." This time the voice directed me to read the Bible. I stumbled to the far end of the house seeking a Bible, accompanied by shimmers and sparks of light, much like a flint on a lighter being struck all around me. As I laid my hands on the Bible and pulled it from the shelf, I immediately saw the dark spirits closing in. They surrounded the sparks of light that were surrounding me. I had started to run back to my room when a voice from the light commanded: "Your room stands condemned – enter not into it." So I turned and retreated. I climbed on the king-sized bed and sat down, opening the Bible across my lap. As I attempted to read the Bible for the first time, I found the scriptures hard to read and pronounce out loud. Tears streamed down my cheeks from both the fear and pain that consumed my body. Voices screaming and screeching filled my ears and mind. I thought that at any moment my ears would begin to bleed. A female voice coming from the shimmer of light coached me to keep reading.

Confused and tired, I stopped reading several times, trying to see if this nightmare was over. As soon as my eyes left the pages, darkness would cover my eyes blinding me for a brief moment. Immediately, I would hear and feel the presence of the evil ones around me. Then the voice from the light would speak with a reprimanding tone, "Keep reading."

I kept hearing the evil spirits calling me, tempting me to give up, to stop fighting and submit. They tried to tell me that I wouldn't and couldn't win. They said that my name had been rubbed out of the Book of Life and that my soul belonged to them forever. As night turned to early morning, I struggled to keep reading. I had read the entire book of John, but my mind was incapable of remembering what I had read. As daylight broke, I strained to hold my body up. After three consecutive days without food or sleep, I was exhausted.

As suddenly as the evil spirits appeared, they disappeared. I sat on the bed feeling alone, afraid and confused. My eyes were tired and hurting, but my mind was still raging with crystal meth-amphetamines, prohibiting me from sleeping. I slowly eased off the bed, much like a cat prowling, waiting for something to pounce or come at me.

I eased up the stairs, through the kitchen and into the living room. Seeing nothing that would cause me to retreat, I inched forward slowly. I started down the hall towards my room, and I felt my body cringe with terror. As I entered my room, it appeared dark and gloomy even in the daylight. I crossed over to the far side where my bed and the wall of Wicca stood. The atmosphere of the room literally began to seep into my body, filling me with gloom and despair. I looked around seeing nothing of real importance. My vision was altered and shaky from the lack of sleep. I scared myself several times, jumping, thinking something was after me. It was only my eyes twitching, and I continued with my search of the room.

As the day continued, so did my fears and uncertainties. I sat for hours trying to rationalize my experience. I tried to convince myself that it was the drugs, concluding it was a bad trip. Even better, perhaps I simply had lost my mind and snapped otherwise known as wigging out. However, I was not able to convince myself. Regardless, I tried to move forward with the day. I did manage to drink some fluids but still was unable to eat. I laid down several times but couldn't sleep. Finally, sitting on the couch, the day slipped away into the night.

With the new night came further disaster. As I sat, feeling tired and ready to fall asleep, I looked up and began to see things move around as they had the night before. First one appeared, then a second. Everything I had experienced the night before started over again, only this time it was much worse. I could feel the evil spirits touch me, causing my skin to crawl. Crying out once more, I was told to read.

I tried to remember where I had turned to in the Bible the night before but struggled to recall. While fumbling through the pages, I tried to keep moving, putting distance between the unclean spirits and myself. Repeatedly I was shaken at the feeling of one of the males successfully sneaking up behind me and causing the feel of penetration to run throughout my body. Time quickly passed and I found myself losing all hope, energy and desire to keep going. Eventually I collapsed on the couch where I gave up and gave in. I felt my nose began to run but did not realize it was drops of blood until my eyes caught sight of the drops hitting the pages of the Bible.

Tears filled my eyes as a renewed willingness to accept my fate came upon me. I found myself no longer afraid—no longer upset or wanting to bargain. My last words were, "Lord God, please forgive me. I never knew." With humbled tears in my eyes and a sigh of relief, I felt my body begin to slide off the couch and then hit the floor. I closed my eyes, drawing in what I thought was going to be my last dying breath. Seconds passed as I lay waiting, but nothing happened. Slowly the pains began to slip away. The consuming fear I had began to fade away as well. I slowly opened my eyes not knowing what to expect. In the distance, shadows of lost souls still danced from one corner of the room to another. As my eyes searched for answers, I began to see the outline of a male. I realized he was different than the other beings that had been in the room. As I embraced his presence, I began to hear a soft voice whisper, "You are forgiven. Now live for Me."

That night my cries turned to wails as I, for the first time in my life, came to know and experience the love of our Lord. In His desire to see me set free, He had turned me over to the very hands of the enemy—knowing it would be the only thing that would save me from this world and myself.

I wish I could tell you that after that night I never did anything else wrong. If I did, it would be a lie. My life did take an immediate change of direction, though. I removed all of the Wicca and drug paraphernalia that occupied my room. I also removed a large collection of pornographic material and homosexual memorabilia.

I took everything I had removed from the room and set it on fire. I watched evidence of my life's previous existence go up in smoke, including all my pictures of old friends, vacations and my teenage years. I watched as everything from my past disappeared. It wasn't easy for me. I actually felt as if in some way I was dying at that very moment. Looking back now I realize I was dying—a death of the old self. After the fire, my life began to change dramatically for the good. Happiness became a part of my life, replacing the old feelings of hopelessness. I actually wanted to live instead of die.

When you make the same change in your life as I did, it's not the end, but just the beginning. I encourage you not to allow your beginning to be the end. I pray each and every one of you will find the strength to take the next step the Lord requires of you as He begins to conform you to His image. Your success will depend on you making choices to separate yourself from your past, closing the door on the old ways and adopting His ways, which result in life instead of death.

First to those in Damascus, then to those in Jerusalem and in all Judea, and to the Gentiles also, I preached that they should repent and turn to God and prove their repentance by their deeds.
ACTS 26:20

What benefit did you reap at that time from the things you are now ashamed of?
ROMANS 6:21

The Lord will give you strength, love, and guidance. He already knows that you may stumble and you might even fall. However, if you keep trying to walk in His ways, He will be faithful and true to you. Nevertheless there is one catch…

You have to know His ways! I encourage you to pick up a Study Bible. I highly recommend the New International Version translation (NIV) because I find that it is much easier to understand.

Don't get confused with denominations and, more importantly, don't get caught up in all of their man-made doctrines and theologies. Read the uncompromised Word of God and test everyone's opinion by how it lines up with the Bible. Concerning the gifts of the spirit and the speaking of tongues, I assure you they both are very real and are very much a part of who Christ is, both then and today. Please stay away from people who speak negatively. The seed that they sow is poisoned.

See to it that no one takes you captive through hollow and deceptive philosophy, which depends on human tradition and the basic principles of this world rather than on Christ.
COLOSSIANS 2:8

Without question, stay clear of those who say they are saved but live as if they are not. They might call themselves backslidden, but I call them wolves in sheep's clothing.

Jesus speaking:
> **"Not everyone who says to me, 'Lord, Lord,' will enter the kingdom of heaven, but only he who does the will of my Father who is in heaven. Many will say to me on that day, 'Lord, Lord, did we not prophesy in your name, and in your name drive out demons and perform many miracles?' Then I will tell them plainly, ' I never knew you. Away from me, you evildoers!'**
> MATTHEW 7:21-23

I protect my soul and my spirit from this world and its temptations no matter the cost. I personally made a choice to refuse to listen to secular music of any kind. I even went as far as to destroy all the CDs I had at the time. This might sound extreme to some, but it was completely necessary for my own success. Television had been a major part of my life as well, but now I limit it, too. I no longer feed my flesh with shows that contain profanity, nudity, spell casting, and/or demon hunting. As you know from my testimony, I've had my fill of all of those things. My days of hunting for vampires and charmed ones are forever over.

> **So we fix our eyes not on what is seen, but on what is unseen. For what is seen is temporary, but what is unseen is eternal.**
> 2ND CORINTHIANS 4:18

I keep a very tight leash on who I allow into my life. In all honesty, I have very few friends left. This personally has proven to be one of the hardest but most beneficial choices I've made. I've learned to keep people at a distance, especially when it comes to those who refuse to accept my Salvation or even believe in my ability to change. Sadly, I've even discovered to use caution when it comes to certain churchgoers. Not everyone is where you are or is willing to understand where you come from. Nor is everyone who attends church saved; so be careful. I encourage you to find a church you feel comfortable in and attend regularly. The Lord will lead you as you listen to His voice. Remember that Sunday is not the only day you can attend church either. The more you go, the easier you will find life to be. In time, the Lord will direct friends into your life. When they come, they will come with love, respect, and sincerity. So, wait on Him!

> **All the believers were together and had everything in common. Selling their possessions and goods, they gave to anyone as he had need. *Every day they continued to meet together in the temple courts.* They broke bread in their homes and ate together with glad and sincere hearts, praising God and enjoying the favor of all the people. And the Lord added to their number *daily* those who were being saved.**
>
> ACTS 2:44-47, EMPHASIS ADDED

> **And let us consider how we may spur one another on toward love and good deeds. *Let us not give up meeting together, as some are***

**in the habit of doing, but let us encourage
one another – and all the more as you see
the Day approaching.**
HEBREWS 10:24-25, EMPHASIS ADDED

**Do not be yoked together with unbelievers.
For what do righteousness and wickedness
have in common? Or what fellowship can
light have with darkness? What harmony
is there between Christ and Belial? What
does a believer have in common with an
unbeliever?**
2ND CORINTHIANS 6:14-15

For the next several weeks you'll see improvements,
but you'll also have trials and temptations. I can guar-
antee you that people you haven't seen or heard from in
ages will come out of the woodwork—including that
person you still have feelings for. Stand your ground
and pull through each circumstance the best you can.
Keep in mind that you're now working towards true love,
friendship and eternity.

**To those who by persistence in doing good
seek glory, honor and immortality, he will
give eternal life.**
ROMANS 2:7

That pain and depression you will feel during this time
will end. Then joy will come as a reward for your obedience, but you must be obedient! Make up whatever
excuses you have to, but separate yourself from your past
and even those friends that would link you to it.

Consider it pure joy, my brothers, whenever you face trials of many kinds, because you know that the testing of your faith develops perseverance. Perseverance must finish its work so that you may be mature and complete, not lacking anything.
JAMES 1:2

Blessed is the man who perseveres under trial, because when he has stood the test, he will receive the crown of life that God has promised to those who love him.
JAMES 1:12

When tempted, no one should say, "God is tempting me." For God cannot be tempted by evil, nor does he tempt anyone; but each one is tempted when, by his own evil desire, he is dragged away and enticed. Then, after desire has conceived, it gives birth to sin; and sin, when it is full grown, gives birth to death.
JAMES 1:13-15

Dear friends, do not be surprised at the painful trial you are suffering, as though something strange were happening to you. But *rejoice* that you participate in the sufferings of Christ, so that you may be overjoyed when his glory is revealed.
1ST PETER 4:12-13, EMPHASIS ADDED

You have a long road ahead of you, a road that leads down a straight and narrow path. It's a path you will find in the beginning often filled with tough decisions and painful sacrifice. But without question, it's a path that is filled with greater joy and happiness than you will be able to imagine. More importantly, it's a path that leads to a Man, perfect in love, patience and kindness, waiting for and wanting you. A Man who will lead, guide and protect you through any and all of your confusion. He's a Man who will always be faithful and dependable, who offers you a relationship that will truly last for all of eternity.

My love goes out to each of you. May the Day of Judgment bring us together forever.

Your friend and Brother,
Shanahn C. Smith

Q&A *with the Author*

1. Do you believe it is possible to completely overcome homosexuality?

I believe that it's not only possible but guaranteed! The word of the Lord promises us that when we repent and turn from our sins, we find forgiveness and life everlasting. In that life, we find newness of creation, which simply means that our spirit has a rebirth – becoming a new person. (Romans 8:1-2) With the rebirth of our spirit, we find empowerment from on High that drives us from the darkness of our past failures to the brightness of our future. The things we once were driven by become the things we now hate and flee from. Conviction now becomes the new driving force. It must be noted, however, that while the rebirth of our spirit is immediate upon Salvation, our "growing in faith" is a work in progress. Each day the newly born-again believer will find that he or she will have to make choices that will be difficult but rewarding. However, the believer must make the right choices if he or she truly desires to be free. The great thing about rebirth is that the Holy Spirit will enlighten and convict you concerning your wrong choices, ever so gently leading you in the path of righteousness for His name's sake. In the end, you have someone, like myself, who has overcome the bondage of a broken sexual image.

2. What do you believe is the key we've been missing?

Exactly! The key that "we've", the Church and fellow Christians, have been missing is Love. The church, in its ignorance and spiritual immaturity, has been totally missing it for years because of hate and fear and hypocritical and judgmental attitudes. We've been so determined to throw stones that we've forgotten about our own sins and failures, leaving us without compassion and understanding. In simpler words, the church has been overtaken by religion. Unfortunately, religion in the church is something that has been around since the beginning and will, without question, linger until the day of the second coming. Nevertheless, religion is a sin no different than homosexuality, and many Christians struggle with it. So, why are we not throwing those who struggle with religion out of our churches? Because pride is the root of religion and the blindness that follows is more deadly than sodomy. If you don't believe me just ask Jesus. You see, religion is the very thing that hung Him on the cross. It came in the form of the Pharisees and Sadducees.

Love is patient, love is kind. It does not envy, it does not boast, it is not proud. It is not rude, it is not self-seeking, it is not eas-

ily angered, it keeps no record of wrongs. Love does not delight in evil but rejoices with the truth. It always protects, always trusts, always hopes, always perseveres. Love never fails.

1st CORINTHIANS 13:4-8, NIV

3. Why do so few, seemingly, achieve victory in this area?

Two words: Desire and Relationship.

It is impossible to do anything without a personal relationship with our Heavenly Father through Jesus Christ. However, because of the effects religion has had on the church, few actually understand and posses this. You simply cannot go to church on Sunday and live like Hell Monday through Saturday and expect to ever achieve anything other than damnation. A relationship with our Heavenly Father and His Son Jesus Christ comes at a high price, and it takes sacrifice and time, which are both priceless in this current age. Sadly, telling a believer to do something as simple as turning off the television and picking up the Bible is like telling a heroin addict to "simply" quit shooting up after twelve years of addiction. On the other hand, that's exactly what is required! Anyone who is truly seeking freedom from sin must understand that it takes time and effort. Because of the time and effort that's required, without desire it will be absolutely impossible for an individual to have any type of victory. You must always remember that your "wants" will never carry you but your desire will. What is the difference between want and desire, you might ask. Passion! Each one of us is inundated daily with things that we want, with most being things that we will never posses. But our desires are the things that drive us to succeed. It's what we wake up each day longing for and intending to achieve. When we place our desires on a personal relationship with our Heavenly Father through Christ Jesus, we have victory because we have life, because He is the author of life.

4. What are some important new behavior patterns to acquire when overcoming sexual confusion?

> **For you were once darkness, but now you are light in the Lord. Walk as children of light. (for the fruit of the Spirit is in all goodness, righteousness, and truth), finding out what is acceptable to the Lord. And have no fellowship with the unfruitful works of darkness, but rather expose them. For it is shameful even to speak of those things which are done by them in secret.**
> EPHESIANS 5:8-12, NKJV

> **But the fruit of the Spirit is love, joy, peace, longsuffering, kindness, goodness, faithfulness, gentleness, self-control...**
> GALATIANS 5:22-23, NKJV

> **Do not let any unwholesome talk come out of your mouths, but only what is helpful for building others up according to their needs, that it may benefit those who listen.**
> EPHESIANS 4:29, NIV

> **Get rid of all bitterness, rage and anger, brawling and slander, along with every form of malice. Be kind and compassionate to one another, forgiving each other, just as in Christ God forgave you.**
> EPHESIANS 4:31-32, NIV

> **Be imitators of God, therefore as dearly loved children and live a life of love, just as Christ loved us and gave himself up for us as a fragrant offering and sacrifice to God.**
> EPHESIANS 5:1-2, NIV

> **But among you there must not be even a hint of sexual immorality, or of any kind of impurity, or of greed, because these are improper for God's holy people. Nor should there be obscenity, foolish talk or coarse joking, which are out of place, but rather thanksgiving.**
> EPHESIANS 5:3-4, NIV

5. How can parents, teachers and pastors better communicate with those desiring help with sexual confusion?

> **My people are destroyed for lack of knowledge. Because you have rejected knowledge, I also will reject you from being priest for Me; Because you have forgotten the law of your God, I also will forget your children**
> HOSEA 4:6 NKJV

Knowledge backed with God-given wisdom is the only answer I can give for any leader or layperson who is seeking to help those dealing with sexual brokenness. You must have a God-given understanding that can only come from personal time spent in the presence of the Lord and His Word. There are also other books like this that can give further insight to understanding sexual brokenness, those who struggle with it, and those who have overcome it.

When a leader is presented with a case of sexual brokenness for the first time, one must remember it's not a quick fix, nor should it be presented as one. It's a very complicated issue that too many wish to express their personal opinions on. These people should simply hold their tongue. One of the most honorable things any leader could ever do is humble themselves in the presence of the Lord and the individual who is struggling and simply say: "I don't know, but let us see if we can find the answer together."

6. What can parents, teachers and pastors do if they notice homosexual tendencies in a child?

This is an area that requires great wisdom and caution. The last thing any child needs is to be placed in a position of recovery before their time or need. Just because a child is experiencing "tendencies" does not mean that child is destined to become a person of an alternative lifestyle. However, what it does mean is that the child is lacking in areas of his life that should be discovered by the leader or parent. Then, compassionately and delicately, the leader should minister to the child in those areas. In most cases, the absence of a proper relationship between the child and his mother or father will be the root of the tendency, but not always. Sometimes the confusion will extend much deeper and without noticeable cause. In some cases, the secrets that are within the child are more spiritual and emotional than physical, often brought on by physical or sexual abuse, rejection, addiction, or even fear, just to name a few. In these cases, the child holds the key, and the mystery can only be unlocked through prayer and supplications from the parents or pastors.

Another word of caution concerning your prayers and the involvement of the child - you need to be aware of the maturity of the child and the degree of his confusion. I would never suggest you involve the actual child in your open prayers concerning his confusion or brokenness unless the child has already become somewhat open to you concerning his confusion. The parents and leaders of the child should take their prayers to the Lord in private, away from the ears of the child. Remember that the enemy is sitting back and waiting for an opportunity to cause the child to feel or become offended, hurt, or even rejected, which I warn will later turn to depression, self-loathing, hate or even suicide. So, once again, wisdom along with your knowledge from personal studies and prayer should be used when dealing with a child showing any "tendencies."

7. How do you respond to critics denouncing your work as prejudice?

And a servant of the Lord must not quarrel but be gentle to all, able to teach, patient, in humility correcting those who are in opposition, if God perhaps will grant them repentance, so that they may know the truth, and that they may come to their senses and escape the snare of the devil, having been taken captive by him to do his will.
2ND TIMOTHY 2:24-26, NKJV

8. How have your sexual desires changed since you committed your life to God?

Today my sexual desires are as different as night and day. But I assure everyone that it definitely didn't happen over night. There were many struggles in my walk, especially in the beginning. One of the worst and most difficult areas of my life was self-control. For years I had cultivated a lifestyle of sexual indulgence, mostly in the area of sexual fantasy and compulsive masturbation. So, by far, this area of my life was the hardest for me to control. It truly dominated my mind and my heart. However, through the power of the Holy Spirit and the conviction He brought to my actions and my thoughts, I was able to slowly break free. The longer I persisted in presenting my body a living sacrifice, the greater I found the presence of God to be in my life. Of course, the greater the presence of God in my life, the greater I found my desire and passion to stay sexually pure. Honestly, there were times of absolute failure. During those times, I felt the sting of a Heavenly Father's disapproval and correction. It only took a couple of failures to know that I wanted His approval, not His discipline. Nevertheless, because of the Lord's persistence in His correction, not forgetting His love, I found freedom from masturbation and lustful fantasies within twelve months of salvation. Currently, I have been free from pornography, sexual fantasies and masturbation for over three years.

9. What materials would you recommend for those who have just completed this book and want to change their lives?

With each passing year, one finds more and more ministries working with and for the sexually broken. Two of the most well known are Exodus International and also Desert Stream Ministries. Both are experienced and well equipped in handling questions concerning sexual wholeness and education. I personally have met and sat under the teachings of Andy Comiskey who is the International Director of Living Waters and the founder and Director of Desert Stream Ministries. After spending a week in a training seminar for Living Waters, I couldn't help but notice the favor and empowerment that God has placed on Andy's life and his ministry. I believe that an individual truly seeking change and desiring to move to the next level of his or her deliverance would be well advised to attend the Living Waters program and check out their other resources. I have found that God's anointing only comes from personal victories of conquest and daily living. From what I witnessed, Andy Comiskey is walking in that anointing.

10. Do you believe God is beginning a new movement – a new standard?

I believe that what we have been seeing concerning the ex-gay movement is just the birth pains of what is to come. Over the years, there has been an ever-increasing number of individuals who have miraculously and successfully broken free from sexual brokenness, including but not limited to, homosexuality and lesbianism.

We have witnessed countless souls delivered, restored, and divinely healed. My question is how can we deny that God has already begun a new movement? He is setting the new standard by His signs, wonders and power as found in the Living Word. His signs and wonders testify to His will and His desire that all should be saved.

Supporting Bible Scriptures

Sexual Immorality

(Old Testament)

Genesis 19:1 – 29

The two angels arrived at Sodom in the evening, and Lot was sitting in the gateway of the city. When he saw them, he got up to meet them and bowed down with his face to the ground. "My lords," he said, "please turn aside to your servant's house. You can wash your feet and spend the night and then go on your way early in the morning."

"No," they answered, "we will spend the night in the square."

But he insisted so strongly that they did go with him and entered his house. He prepared a meal for them, baking bread without yeast, and they ate. Before they had gone to bed, all the men from every part of the city of Sodom – both young and old – surrounded the house. They called to Lot, "where are the men who came to you tonight? Bring them out to us so that we can have sex with them."

Lot went outside to meet them and shut the door behind them and said, "No my friends. Don't do this wicked thing. Look, I have two daughters who have never slept with a man. Let me bring them out to you, and you can do what you like with them. But don't do anything to these men, for they have come under the protection of my roof."

"Get out of our way," they replied. And they said, "This fellow cam here as an alien, and now he wants to play the judge! We'll treat you worse than them." They kept bringing pressure on Lot and moved forward to break down the door. But the men inside reached out and pulled Lot back into the house and shut the door. Then they struck the men who were at the door of the house, young and old, with blindness so that they could not find the door.

The two men said to Lot, "do you have anyone else here – sons-in-law, sons or daughters, or anyone else in the city who belongs to you? Get them out of here, because we are going to destroy this place. They outcry to the Lord against its people is so great that he has sent us to destroy it.

So Lot went out and spoke to his sons-in-law, who were pledged to marry his daughters. He said, "Hurry and get out of this place, because the Lord is about to destroy the city!" But his sons-in-law thought he was joking.

With the coming of dawn, the angels urged Lot, saying, "Hurry! Take your wife and your two daughters who are here, or you will be swept away when the city is punished.

When he hesitated, the men grasped his hand and the hands of his wife and of his two daughters and led them safely out of the city, for the Lord was merciful to them. As soon as they had brought them out, one of them said, "Flee for your lives! Don't look back, and don't stop anywhere in the plain! Flee to the mountains or you will be swept away!

But Lot said them, "No, my lords, please! Your servant has found favor in your eyes, and you have shown great kindness to me in sparing my life. But I can't flee to the mountains; this disaster will overtake me, and I'll die. Look, here is a town near enough to run to, and it is small. Let me flee to it – it is very small, isn't it? Then my life will be spared."

He said to him, "Very well, I will grant this request too; I will not over throw the town you speak of. But flee there quickly, because I cannot do anything until you reach it." (That is why the town was called Zoar.)

By the time Lot reached Zoar, the sun had risen over the land. Then the Lord rained down burning sulfur on Sodom and Gomorrah – from the Lord out of the heavens. Thus he over threw those cities and the entire plain, including all those living in the cities – and also the vegetation in the land. But Lot's wife looked back, and she became a pillar of salt.

Early the next morning Abraham got up and returned to the place where he had stood before the Lord. He looked down toward Sodom and Gomorrah, toward all the land of the plain, and he saw dense smoke rising from the land, like smoke from a furnace. So when God destroyed the cities of the plain, he remembered Abraham, and he brought Lot out of the catastrophe that overthrew the cities where Lot had lived.

Deuteronomy 22:5

A woman must not wear men's clothing, nor a man wear women's clothing, for the Lord your God detests anyone who does this.

Leviticus 18:22

Do not lie with a man as one lies with a woman; that is detestable.

Leviticus 20:13

If a man lies with a man as one lies with a woman, both of them have done what is detestable. They must be put to death; their blood will be on their own heads.

* Through Christ Jesus, when we repent, we are now forgiven and have freedom from such sin. Death is no longer required from the individual. This is the blessing of the New Testament.

(New Testament)

Mark 7:20-23

He went on: "What comes out of a man is what makes him "unclean." For from within, out of men's hearts, come evil thoughts, sexual immorality, theft, murder, adultery, greed, malice, deceit, lewdness, envy, slander, arrogance and folly. All these evils come from inside and make a man "unclean".

Romans 1:18-32

The Wrath of God is being revealed from heaven against all the Godlessness and wickedness of men who suppress the truth by their wickedness, since what may be known about God is plain to them, because God has made it plain to them. For since the creation of the world God's invisible qualities – His eternal power and divine nature – have been clearly seen, being understood from what has been made, so that men are without excuse. For although they knew God, they neither glorified him as God nor gave thanks to him, but their thinking became futile and their foolish hearths were darkened. Although they clamed to be wise, they became fools and exchanged the glory of the immortal God for images made to look like mortal man and birds and animals and reptiles. Therefore God gave them over in the sinful desires of their hearts to sexual impurity for the degrading of their bodies with one another. They exchanged the truth of God for a lie, and worshiped and served created things rather than the Creator – who is forever praised. Amen. Because of this, God gave them over to shameful lust, even their women exchanged natural relations for unnatural ones. In the same way the men also abandoned natural relations with women and were inflamed with lust for one another. Men committed indecent acts with other men, and received in themselves the due penalty for the perversion. Furthermore, since they did not think it worthwhile to retain the knowledge of God, he gave them over to a depraved mind, to do what ought not to be done. They have become filled with every kind of wickedness, evil, greed and depravity. They are full of envy, murder, strife, deceit and malice. They are gossips, slanderers, God-haters, insolent, arrogant and boastful; they invent ways of doing evil; they disobey their parents; they are senseless, faithless, heartless, ruthless. Although they know God's righteous decree that those who do such things deserve death, they not only continue to do these very things but also approve of those who practice them.

Romans 2:5-11, NLT

But because you are stubborn and refuse to turn from your sin, you are storing up terrible punishment for yourself. For a day of anger is coming, when God's righteous judgment will be revealed. He will judge everyone according to what they have done. He will give eternal life to those who keep on doing good, seeking after the glory and honor and immortality that God offers. But he will pour out his anger and wrath on those who live for themselves, who refuse to obey the truth and instead live lives of wickedness. There will be trouble and calamity for everyone who keeps on doing what is evil – for the Jew first and also for the Gentile. But there will be glory and honor and peace from God for all who do good – for the Jew first and also for the Gentile. For God does not show favoritism.

1st Corinthians 5:9-11

I have written you in my letter not to associate with sexually immoral people – not at all meaning the people of this world who are immoral, or that greedy and swindlers, or idolaters. In that case you would have to leave this world. But now I am writing you that you must not associate with anyone who calls himself a brother but is sexually immoral or greedy, an idolater or a slanderer, a drunkard or a swindler. With such a man do not even eat.

1st Corinthians 6:9-11

Do you not know that the Wicked will not inherit the kingdom of God? Do not be deceived: Neither the sexually immoral nor idolaters nor adulterers nor male prostitutes nor homosexual offenders nor thieves nor the greedy nor drunkards nor slanderers nor swindlers will inherit the kingdom of God. And that is what some of you were. But you were washed, you were sanctified, you were justified in the name of the Lord Jesus Christ and by the spirit of our God.

1st Corinthians 6:13b

The body is not meant for sexual immorality, but for the Lord, and the Lord for the body.

1st Corinthians 6:18-20

Flee from sexual immorality. All other sins a man commits are outside his body, but he who sins sexually sins against his own body. Do you not know that your body is a temple of the Holy Spirit, who is in you, whom you have received from God? You are not your own; you were bought at a price. Therefore honor God with you body.

1st Corinthians 10:1-11, NLT

I don't want you to forget, dear brothers and sisters, about our ancestors in the wilderness long ago. All of them were guided by a cloud that moved ahead of them, and all of them walked through the sea on dry ground. In the cloud and in the sea, all of them were baptized as followers of Moses. All of them ate the same spiritual food, and all of them drank the same spiritual water. For they drank from the spiritual rock that traveled with them, and that rock was Christ. Yet God was not pleased with most of them, and their bodies were scattered in the wilderness. These things happened as a warning to us, so that we would not crave evil things as they did, or worship idols as some of them did. As the Scriptures say, "The people celebrated with feasting and drinking, and they indulged in pagan revelry." And we must not engage in sexual immorality as some of them did, causing 23,000 of them to die in one day. Nor should we put Christ to the test, as some of them did and then died from snakebites. And don't grumble as some of them did, and then were destroyed by the angel of death. These things happened to them as examples for us. They were written down to warn us who live at the end of the age.

Galatians 5:19-21

The acts of the sinful nature are obvious: sexual immorality, impurity and debauchery; idolatry and witchcraft; hatred, discord, jealousy, fits of rage, selfish ambition, dissensions, factions and envy; drunkenness, orgies, and the like. I warn you, as I did before, that those who live like this will not inherit the kingdom of God.

1st Thessalonians 4:1-5, NLT

Finally, dear brothers and sisters, we urge you in the name of the Lord Jesus to live in a way that pleases God, as we have taught you. You live this way already, and we encourage you to do so even more. For you remember what we taught you by the authority of the Lord Jesus. God's will is for you to be holy, so stay away from all sexual sin. Then each of you will control his own body and live in holiness and honor – not in lustful passion like the pagans who do not know God and his ways.

Hebrews 12:14-17

Make every effort to live in peace with all men and to be holy; without holiness no one will see the Lord. See to it that no one misses the grace of God and that no bitter root grows up to cause trouble and defile many. See that no one is sexually immoral, or is godless like Esau, who for a single meal sold his inheritance rights as the oldest son. Afterward, as you know, when he wanted to inherit this blessing, he was rejected. He could bring about no change of mind, though he sought the blessing with tears.

Hebrews 13:4, The Message

Honor marriage, and guard the sacredness of sexual intimacy between wife and husband. God draws a firm line against casual and illicit sex.

Substance Abuse and Drug Addictions

(Old Testament)

Proverbs 23:20-21

Do not join those who drink too much wine or gorge themselves on meat, for drunkards and gluttons become poor, and drowsiness clothes them in rags.

Proverbs 20:1

Wine is a mocker, Strong drink is a brawler, And whoever is led astray by it is not wise.

1st Thessalonians 5:4-11, The Message

But friends, you're not in the dark, so how could you be taken off guard by any of this? You're sons of Light, daughters of Day. We live under wide open skies and know where we stand. So let's not sleepwalk through life like those others. Let's keep our eyes open and be smart. People sleep at night and get drunk at night. But not us! Since we're creatures of Day, let's act like it. Walk out into the daylight sober, dressed up in faith, love, and the hope of salvation.

God didn't set us up for an angry rejection but for salvation by our Master, Jesus Christ. He died for us, a death that triggered life. Whether we're awake with the living or asleep with the dead, we're alive with him! So speak encouraging words to one another. Build up hope so you'll all be together in this, no one left out, no one left behind. I know you're already doing this; just keep on doing it.

(New Testament)

Ephesians 5:15-18
Be very careful, then, how you live – not as unwise but as wise, making the most of every opportunity, because the days are evil. Therefore do not be foolish, but understand what the Lord's will is. Do not get drunk on wine, which leads to debauchery. Instead, be filled with the Spirit.

1st Thessalonians 5:8-9, AMP
But we belong to the day; therefore, let us be sober and put on the breastplate (corslet) of faith and love and for a helmet the hope of salvation. For God has not appointed us to [incur His] wrath [He did not select us to condemn us], but [that we might] obtain [His] salvation through our Lord Jesus Christ (the Messiah)

Titus 2:6-7

Similarly, encourage the young men to be self-controlled. In everything set them an example by doing what is good.

Titus 2:11-14

For the grace of God that brings salvation has appeared to all men. It teaches us to say "No" to ungodliness and worldly passions, and to live self-controlled, upright and godly lives in this present age, while we wait for the blessed hope – the glorious appearing of our great God and Savior, Jesus Christ, who gave himself for us to redeem us from all wickedness and to purify for himself a people that are his very own, eager to do what is good.

1st Peter 1:13-16

Therefore, prepare your minds for action; be self-controlled; set your hope fully on the grace to be given you when Jesus Christ is revealed. As obedient children, do not conform to the evil desires you had when you lived in ignorance. But just as he who called you is holy, so be holy in all you do; for it is written: "Be holy, because I am holy."

1st Peter 4:7

The end of all things is near. Therefore be clear minded and self-controlled so that you can pray.

1st Peter 5:8, KJV

Be sober, be vigilant; because your adversary the devil, as a roaring lion, walketh about, seeking whom he may devour.

Witchcraft

(*Including but not limited to: Satanist, mediums, spiritualist, pagan followers, physics, astrologers, Christian witches and all forms of the New Age moment.)

(Old Testament)

Exodus 20:3, Emphasis Added
From the Ten Commandments

You shall have no other Gods before me. You shall not make for yourself an idol in the form of anything in heaven above or on the earth beneath or in the waters below. You shall not bow down to them or worship them; for I, the Lord your God, am a *Jealous* God.

* *Jealous: Demanding exclusive devotion to Himself, putting up with no rivalry for your attention or faithfulness*

Exodus 22:18
Do not allow a sorceress to live

Leviticus 19:26
The Lord speaking to Moses said:
"Do not practice divination or sorcery."

Leviticus 19:31, KJV
The Lord speaking to Moses said:
Regard not them that have familiar spirits, neither seek after wizards, to be defiled by them: I am the Lord.

Leviticus 20:6
The Lord speaking to Moses said:
I will set my face against the person who turns to mediums and spiritists to prostitute himself by following them, and I will cut him off from his people.

Leviticus 20:27, AMP
The Lord speaking to Moses said:
A man or woman who is a medium and has a familiar spirit or is a wizard shall surely be put to death, be stoned with stones; their blood shall be upon them.

Deuteronomy 18:9-13
When you enter the land the Lord your God is giving you, do not learn to imitate the detestable ways for the nations there. Let no one be found among you who sacrifices his son or daughters in the fire, who practices divination or sorcery, interprets omens, engages in witchcraft, or casts spells or who is a medium or spiritists or who consults the dead. Anyone who does these things is detestable to the Lord, and because of these detestable practices the Lord your God will drive out those nations before you. You must be blameless before the Lord your God.

2nd Kings 21:1-6
Manasseh was twelve years old when he became king, and he reigned in Jerusalem fifty-five years. His mother's name was Hephzibah. He did evil in the eyes of the LORD, following the detestable practices of the nations the LORD had driven out before the Israelites. He rebuilt the high places his father Hezekiah had destroyed; he also erected altars to Baal and made an Asherah pole, as Ahab king of Israel had done. He bowed down to all the starry hosts and worshiped them. He built altars in the

temple of the LORD, of which the LORD had said, "In Jerusalem I will put my Name." In both courts of the temple of the LORD, he built altars to all the starry hosts. He sacrificed his own son in the fire, practiced sorcery and divination, and consulted mediums and spiritists. He did much evil in the eyes of the LORD, provoking him to anger.

2nd Kings 21:11-15

"Manasseh king of Judah has committed these detestable sins. He has done more evil than the Amorites who preceded him and has led Judah into sin with his idols. Therefore this is what the LORD, the God of Israel, says: I am going to bring such disaster on Jerusalem and Judah that the ears of everyone who hears of it will tingle.

2nd Kings 23:4-5, AMP

And the king commanded Hilkiah the high priest and the priests of the second rank and the keepers of the threshold to bring out of the temple of the Lord all the vessels made for Baal, for [the goddess] Asherah, and for all the hosts of the heavens; and he burned them outside Jerusalem in the fields of the Kidron, and carried their ashes to Bethel [where Israel's idolatry began]. [1st Kings 12:28,29.] He put away the idolatrous priests whom the kings of Judah had ordained to burn incense in the high places in Judah's cities and round about Jerusalem – also those who burned incense to Baal, to the sun, to the moon, to the constellations [or twelve signs of the zodiac], and to all the hosts of the heavens.

2nd Kings 23:24-26, AMP

Moreover, Josiah put away the mediums, the wizards, the teraphim (household gods), the idols, and all the abominations that were seen in Judah and in Jerusalem, that he might establish the words of the law written in the book found by Hilkiah the priest in the house of the Lord. There was no king like him before or after [Josiah] who turned to the Lord with all his heart and all his soul and all his might, according to all the Law of Moses. Still the Lord did not turn from the fierceness of His great wrath, kindled against Judah because of all the provocations with which Manasseh had provoked Him.

Isaiah 19:1-4, AMP

The Mournful, inspired prediction (a burden to be lifted up) concerning Egypt: Behold, the Lord is riding on a swift cloud and comes to Egypt; and the idols of Egypt will tremble at His presence, and the hearts of the Egyptians will melt within them. And I will stir up Egyptians against Egyptians, and they will fight, every one against his brother and every one against his neighbor, city against city, kingdom against kingdom. And the spirit of the Egyptians within them will become exhausted and emptied out and will fail, and I will destroy their counsel and confound their plans; and they will seek counsel from the idols and the sorcerers, and from those having familiar spirits (the mediums) and the wizards. And I will give over the Egyptians into the hand of a hard and cruel master, and a fierce king will rule over them, says the Lord, the Lord of hosts.

Isaiah 8:19-22

When men tell you to consult mediums and spiritists, who whisper and muster, should not a people inquire of the God? Why consult the dead on behalf of the living? To the law and to the testimony! If they do not speak according to this word, they have no light of dawn. Distressed and hungry, they will roam through the land; when they are famished, they will become enraged and, looking upward, will curse their king and their God. They will look toward the earth and see only distress and darkness and fearful gloom, and they will be thrust into utter darkness.

Also translated:

Isaiah 8:19-22 The Message

When people tell you, "Try out the fortunetellers. Consult the spiritualists. Why not tap into the spirit-world, get in touch with the dead?" Tell them, "No, we're going to study the Scriptures." People who try the other ways get nowhere—a dead end! Frustrated and famished, they try one thing after another. When nothing works out they get angry, cursing first this god and then that one, Looking this way and that, up, down, and sideways—and seeing nothing, A blank wall, an empty hole. They end up in the dark with nothing.

Isaiah 47:11

A prophet of the Lord speaking on God's behalf concerning the judgment that will soon come upon Babylon:

Disaster will come upon you, and you will not know how to conjure it away. A calamity will fall upon you that you cannot ward off with a ransom; a catastrophe you cannot foresee will suddenly come upon you. "Keep on, then, with your magic spells and with your many sorceries, which you have labored at since childhood. Perhaps you will succeed, perhaps you will cause terror. All the counsel you have received has only worn you out! Let your astrologers come forward, those star-gazers who make predictions month by month, let them save you from what is coming upon you. Surely they are like stubble; the fire will burn them up. They cannot even save themselves from the power of the flame. Here are no coals to warm anyone; here is no fire to sit by. That is all they can do for you – these you have labored with and trafficked with since childhood. Each of them goes on in his error; there is not one that can save you.

1st Chronicles 10:13-14

Saul died because he was unfaithful to the Lord; he did not keep the word of the Lord and even consulted a medium for guidance, and did not inquire of the Lord. So the Lord put him to death and turned the kingdom over to David son of Jesse.

2nd Chronicles 33:2 -6

Ezra the author of Chronicles speaking on Manasseh king of Judah as originally told in 2nd Kings 21:1-6

Manasseh was twelve years old when he became king, and he reigned in Jerusalem fifty-five years. He did evil in the eyes of the Lord, following the detestable practices of the nations the Lord had driven out before the Israelites. He rebuilt the high places his father Hezekiah had demolished; he also erected altars to the Baals and made Asherah plies. He bowed down to all the starry hosts and worshiped them. He built altars in the temple of the Lord, of which the Lord had said, "My Name will remain in Jerusalem forever." In both courts of the temple of the Lord, He built altars to all the starry hosts. He sacrificed his sons in the fire in the Valley of Ben Hinnom, practiced sorcery, divination and witchcraft, and consulted mediums and spiritists. He did much evil in the eyes of the Lord, provoking him to anger.

Jeremiah 8:1-3
The Lord Almighty speaking to His prophet Jeremiah concerning the people of Judah

"At that time, declares the Lord, the bones of the kings and officials of Judah, the bones of the priests and prophets, and the bones of the people of Jerusalem will be removed from their graves. They will be exposed to the sun and the moon and all the stars of the heavens, which they have loved and served and which they have followed and consulted and worshiped. They will not be gathered up or buried, but will be like refuse lying on the ground. Wherever I banish them, all the survivors of this evil nation will prefer death to life, declares the Lord Almighty."

Daniel 2:1 -49; The Message
This is the story of King Nebuchadnezzar and his dream. It should be noted that no matter how hard the magicians, enchanters, sorcerers, and astrologers tried to interpret the king's dream, they could not. Ultimately the dream was interpreted by a true man of God revealing the lack of knowledge and power astrologers and sorcerers have. All power and knowledge comes from God and no other.

In the second year of his reign, King Nebuchadnezzar started having dreams that disturbed him deeply. He couldn't sleep. He called in all the Babylonian magicians, enchanters, sorcerers, and fortunetellers to interpret his dreams for him. When they came and lined up before the king, he said to them, "I had a dream that I can't get out of my mind. I can't sleep until I know what it means."

The fortunetellers, speaking in the Aramaic language, said, "Long live the king! Tell us the dream and we will interpret it."

The king answered the fortunetellers, "This is my decree: If you can't tell me both the dream itself and its interpretation, I'll have you ripped to pieces, limb from limb, and your homes torn down. But if you tell me both the dream and its interpretation, I'll lavish you with gifts and honors. So go to it: Tell me the dream and its interpretation."

They answered, "If it please your majesty, tell us the dream. We'll give the interpretation."

But the king said, "I know what you're up to—you're just playing for time. You know you're up a tree. You know that if you can't tell me my dream, you're doomed. I see right through you—you're going to cook up some fancy stories and confuse the issue until I change my mind. Nothing doing! First tell me the dream, then I'll know that you're on the up and up with the interpretation and not just blowing smoke in my eyes."

The fortunetellers said, "Nobody anywhere can do what you ask. And no king, great or small, has ever demanded anything like this from any magician, enchanter, or fortuneteller. What you're asking is impossible unless some god or goddess should reveal it—and they don't hang around with people like us."

That set the king off. He lost his temper and ordered the whole company of Babylonian wise men killed. When the death warrant was issued, Daniel and his companions were included. They also were marked for execution.

When Arioch, chief of the royal guards, was making arrangements for the execution, Daniel wisely took him aside and quietly asked what was going on: "Why this all of a sudden?"

After Arioch filled in the background, Daniel went to the king and asked for a little time so that he could interpret the dream.

Daniel then went home and told his companions Hananiah, Mishael, and Azariah what was going on. He asked them to pray to the God of heaven for mercy in solving this mystery so that the four of them wouldn't be killed along with the whole company of Babylonian wise men.

Dream Interpretation: A Story of Five Kingdoms

That night the answer to the mystery was given to Daniel in a vision. Daniel blessed the God of heaven, saying,

"Blessed be the name of God,
forever and ever.
He knows all, does all:
He changes the seasons and guides history,
He raises up kings and also brings them down,
he provides both intelligence and discernment,
He opens up the depths, tells secrets,
sees in the dark—light spills out of him!
God of all my ancestors, all thanks! all praise!
You made me wise and strong.
And now you've shown us what we asked for.
You've solved the king's mystery."

So Daniel went back to Arioch, who had been put in charge of the execution. He said, "Call off the execution! Take me to the king and I'll interpret his dream."

Arioch didn't lose a minute. He ran to the king, bringing Daniel with him, and said, "I've found a man from the exiles of Judah who can interpret the king's dream!"

The king asked Daniel (renamed in Babylonian, Belteshazzar), "Are you sure you can do this—tell me the dream I had and interpret it for me?"

Daniel answered the king, "No mere human can solve the king's mystery, I don't care who it is—no wise man, enchanter, magician, diviner. But there is a God in heaven who solves mysteries, and he has solved this one. He is letting King Nebuchadnezzar in on what is going to happen in the days ahead. This is the dream you had when you were lying on your bed, the vision that filled your mind:

"While you were stretched out on your bed, O king, thoughts came to you regarding what is coming in the days ahead. The Revealer of Mysteries showed you what will happen. But the interpretation is given through me, not because I'm any smarter than anyone else in the country, but so that you will know what it means, so that you will understand what you dreamed.

"What you saw, O king, was a huge statue standing before you, striking in appearance. And terrifying. The head of the statue was pure gold, the chest and arms were silver, the belly and hips were bronze, 33the legs were iron, and the feet were an iron-ceramic mixture. While you were looking at this statue, a stone cut out of a mountain by an invisible hand hit the statue, smashing its iron-ceramic feet. Then the whole thing fell to pieces—iron, tile, bronze, silver, and gold, smashed to bits. It was like scraps of old newspapers in a vacant lot in a hot dry summer, blown every which way by the wind, scattered to oblivion. But the stone that hit the statue became a huge mountain, dominating the horizon. This was your dream.

"And now we'll interpret it for the king. You, O king, are the most powerful king on earth. The God of heaven has given you the works: rule, power, strength, and glory. He has put you in charge of men and women, wild animals and birds, all over the world—you're the head ruler, you are the head of gold. But your rule will be taken over by another kingdom, inferior to yours, and that one by a third, a bronze kingdom, but still ruling the whole land, and after that by a fourth kingdom, iron-like in strength. Just as iron smashes things to bits, breaking and pulverizing, it will bust up the previous kingdoms.

"But then the feet and toes that ended up as a mixture of ceramic and iron will deteriorate into a mongrel kingdom with some remains of iron in it. Just as the toes of the feet were part ceramic and part iron, it will end up a mixed bag of the breakable and unbreakable. That kingdom won't bond, won't hold together any more than iron and clay hold together.

"But throughout the history of these kingdoms, the God of heaven will be building a kingdom that will never be destroyed, nor will this kingdom ever fall under the domination of another. In the end it will crush the other kingdoms and finish them off and come through it all standing strong and eternal. It will be like the stone cut from the mountain by the invisible hand that crushed the iron, the bronze, the ceramic, the silver, and the gold.

"The great God has let the king know what will happen in the years to come. This is an accurate telling of the dream, and the interpretation is also accurate."

When Daniel finished, King Nebuchadnezzar fell on his face in awe before Daniel. He ordered the offering of sacrifices and burning of incense in Daniel's honor. He said to Daniel, "Your God is beyond question the God of all gods, the Master of all kings. And he solves all mysteries, I know, because you've solved this mystery."

Then the king promoted Daniel to a high position in the kingdom, lavished him with gifts, and made him governor over the entire province of Babylon and the chief in charge of all the Babylonian wise men. At Daniel's request the king appointed Shadrach, Meshach, and Abednego to administrative posts throughout Babylon, while Daniel governed from the royal headquarters.

* Through Christ Jesus, when we repent, we are now forgiven and have freedom from such sin. Death is no longer required from the individual. This is the blessing of the New Testament.

(New Testament)

1st Corinthians 10:19-22
Do I mean then that a sacrifice offered to an idol is anything, or that an idol is anything? No, but the sacrifices of pagans are offered to demons, not to God, and I do not want you to be participants with demons. You cannot drink the cup of the Lord and the cup of demons too; you cannot have a part in both the Lord's table and the table of demons. Are we trying to arouse the Lord's jealousy? Are we stronger than He?

Galatians 5:19-21
The acts of the sinful nature are obvious: sexual immorality, impurity and debauchery; idolatry and witchcraft; hatred, discord, jealousy, fits of rage, self-

ish ambition, dissensions, factions and envy; drunkenness, orgies, and the like. I warn you, as I did before, that those who live like this will not inherit the kingdom of God.

Revelation 21:6-8
God Speaking to John a Prophet and Apostle
He said to me: "It is done. I am the Alpha and the Omega, the Beginning and the End. To him who is thirsty I will give to drink without cost from the spring of the water of life. He who overcomes will inherit all this, and I will be his God and he will be my son. But the cowardly, the unbelieving, the vile, the murderers, the sexually immoral, those who practice magic arts, the idolaters and all liars – their place will be in the fiery lake of burning sulfur. This is the second Death.

Obscene Language and Crude Joking

Ephesians 4:29-32
Do not let any unwholesome talk come out of your mouths, but only what is helpful for building others up according to their needs, that it may benefit those who listen. And do not grieve the Holy Spirit of God, with whom you were sealed for the day of redemption. Get rid of all bitterness, rage and anger, brawling and slander, along with every form of malice. Be kind and compassionate to one another, forgiving each other, just as in Christ God forgave you.

Ephesians 5:4-7
Nor should there be obscenity, foolish talk or coarse joking, which are out of place, but rather thanksgiving. For of this you can be sure: No immoral, impure or

greedy person – such a man is an idolater – has any inheritance in the kingdom of Christ and of God. Let no one deceive you with empty words, for because of such things God's wrath comes on those who are disobedient. Therefore do not be partners with them.

Ephesians 5:19-20

Speak to one another with psalms, hymns and spiritual songs. Sing and make music in your heart to the Lord, always giving thanks to God the Father for everything, in the name of our Lord Jesus Christ.

Philippians 4:8-9

Finally, brothers, whatever is true, whatever is noble, whatever is right, whatever is pure, whatever is lovely, whatever is admirable – if anything is excellent or praiseworthy – think about such things. Whatever you have learned or received or heard from me, or seen in me – put it into practice. And the God of peace will be with you.

Colossians 3:8-10

But now you must rid yourselves of all such things as these: anger, rage, malice, slander, and filthy language from your lips. Do not lie to each other, since you have taken off your old self with its practices and have put on the new self, which is being renewed in knowledge in the image of its Creator.

Titus 2:6-8

In everything set them an example by doing what is good. In your teaching show integrity, seriousness and soundness of speech that cannot be condemned, so that those who oppose you may be ashamed because they have nothing bad to say about us.

Titus 3:9

But avoid foolish controversies and genealogies and arguments and quarrels about the law, because these are unprofitable and useless.

James 1:19-22

My dear brothers, take note of this: Everyone should be quick to listen, slow to speak and slow to become angry, for man's anger does not bring about the righteous life that God desires. Therefore, get rid of all moral filth and the evil that is so prevalent and humbly accept the word planted in you, which can save you. Do not merely listen to the word, and so deceive yourselves. Do what it says.

1st Peter 2:1-3

Therefore, rid yourselves of all malice and all deceit, hypocrisy, envy, and slander of every kind. Like newborn babies, crave pure spiritual milk, so that by it you may grow up in your salvation, now that you have tasted that the Lord is good.

Since the completion of this book...

An update on the Author

I believe that time is like a river, never slowing and constantly flowing. Since the completion of this book, many things have changed. As I look back at the last four years, I can't help but praise the Lord for His mercy and His faithfulness. There are many things that words will never be able to express concerning the revelations He has given me to the love He has shown me. My heart now beams with a glow that only comes from knowing His name. What I would like to do is share about several areas of my life since salvation that I believe were turning points that will bring glory to our Heavenly Father and His Son, Jesus Christ.

Five months after beginning this book, I began to experience several different forms of sickness in my body. What was originally believed to be a cold or the flu seemed only to intensify in various forms over time. Finally after struggling on and off for more than a month

I found myself in the doctor's office after a very bad outbreak that I was certain to be an STD (Sexually Transmitted Disease). I shared very openly and honestly with the physician concerning my previous lifestyle and the testimony of how Christ had set me free. He quickly rejoiced with me but even more quickly ordered every blood test imaginable. On July 7, 2004, I was diagnosed with genital herpes, syphilis, and acute Hepatitis C. Because of the STD's I immediately had to undergo treatment attempting to manage the outbreaks. Because of the seriousness of the outbreaks, I was later treated for a staff infection and had to undergo several rounds of antibiotics along with a series of very painful penicillin shots. But this was only the beginning.

The days ahead were very stressful and even more confusing. I battled to believe that my newly found friend, comforter, and Heavenly Father was still a blessing rather than a disappointment. The enemy attacked with accusations of blame and hopelessness – attempting to set up doubt and offense in my heart. The whispers of why God would only save me to watch me die haunted me in the night and slowly flooded into the day. Some days, my faith was impenetrable as I rejoiced and laughed, believing God for the impossible. Other days were drenched in defeat and doubt as my body began to react to the seriousness of the every-increasing terminal disease. Amazingly, as the days pushed forward so did my faith in God. The more I read the Bible, the more scriptures I found to support that God was a loving and forgiving God, a God of second chances and also of miraculous changes— a God whom I could ultimately trust and would not and could not let me down.

The only thing I couldn't understand at the time was why He was not choosing to heal me instantly (if He loved me)...

In the life of every believer there are times that we, as Christians, will face fears and uncertainties that challenge us to believe that God, in spite of the circumstances, still has our very best interest at heart. These are the times that matter the most.

What we must do is learn to trust in Him and His faithfulness — not leaning to our own understanding, but rather relying on His might, His power, and His Holy Spirit. (Proverbs 3:5 & Zech. 4:6) Where so many of us fail is when we attempt to change our situation by demand rather than faith. We revert back to a carnal way of thinking backed by fear and hurt as we seek out those Bible scriptures that promise us power and change. Then, attempting to force our Heavenly Father to change the situation, we loudly and repeatedly quote that we are Sons of God, heirs of promise. Or even worse, we find ourselves in a shouting match with the devil and every other evil spirit we can put a name on. This is not the way to please our Lord. Faith in God simply believes that, regardless of the situation, God will be there and will see you through it, even if the situation is ultimately more difficult than what you would personally desire for your life or the life of a loved one. We must remember that in the end all things work to the glory of God, to those who are called accordingly. (Romans 8:28) The scriptures also say that God is fully capable of keeping those that are His own. (Romans 8:37)

Your attitude should be the same as that of Christ Jesus: Who, being in very nature God, did not consider equality with God something to be grasped, but made himself nothing, taking the very nature of a servant, being made in human likeness. And being found in appearance as a man, he humbled himself and became obedient to death – even death on a cross! Therefore God exalted him to the highest place and gave him the name that is above every name, that at the name of Jesus every knee should bow, in heaven and on earth and under the earth, and every tongue confess that Jesus Christ is Lord, to the glory of God the Father. (Philippians 2:5-11, NIV)

As the days slowly slipped by, the symptoms of the sickness would appear only to once again disappear. I, out of fear, attempted to find and quote scriptures that would change the outcome of my situation. Unfortunately, each time the symptoms returned, I only found anger and resentment toward God because He had not done what I believed from scripture to be His part. Sadly, this is where we end up when we are weak in faith. God's will is for each of us to be totally healed and delivered. No question! However, it takes endurance of faith to see His desire come to pass. We must be willing to wait, with reassurance, on His timing. (He really does have our best interest at heart).

On August 26, 2004, I found myself in the office of a specialist listening to him proclaim the inevitable. Amazingly enough around the exact same time, my attitude began to change. After a brief examination, the physician began to ask me questions. With excitement I seized the opportunity and begin to tell him my about my previous lifestyle and the testimony of my salvation. I watched as this Indian doctor became both intrigued and uncomfortable. As the minutes ticked by, I watched as my own fears of what he might be thinking of me begin to make me tremble and my voice begin to break. Nevertheless, I pushed forward, attempting my best to present the power of Jesus Christ and His love for me. As I drew to an end I suddenly found myself overcome with nervousness. All I could hear was an internal voice saying, 'He thinks you're a crazed drug addict.' Taking a deep breath, I closed my mouth attempting to gather myself as I waited for His reply.

I really can't recall who was more stunned and speechless. From that moment the conversation slowly faded back into medical terms and actions. His expressed desire from that point was to treat my sickness to the best of his ability. He reassured me that there was no cure and the treatment that would slow the disease would be painful and cause severe depression and possible suicidal tendencies. As he spoke about the treatment plan, I suddenly realized that I was in danger of loosing everything the Lord had just recently given to me. I had waited, what seemed like my entire life, to find happiness and a desire to live, and now as suddenly as I had received it I was going to loose it to a treatment plan that was not going to heal me, but only slow the process. I must confess that before my appointment I had already done some research on the treatment plans and had questioned if they were right for me. At the time, I remember thinking that I was going to boldly proclaim my faith and refuse all treatments in the hopes of a miracle. However, now that I was sitting in the doctor's office hearing about the medications, I was more afraid than bold. So I found myself listening and debating within. As the appointment came to an end, they scheduled some further tests and sent me on my way. Those tests never came to pass. That day, as I walked out of the office I realized that I could not financially afford the tests they had ordered, and I also knew I didn't feel right in my Spirit about taking the treatments. So I made the decision to put my faith and my life in God's hand. I can't begin to tell you how difficult it was for me. I had family and friends who disagreed with me and my decisions. What they didn't say with words, they showed with actions and facial expressions. The truth is, no one in my life had the faith to believe with me. Sadly, this is what most Christians will face at some point in their walk. What you will need to decided is if you're willing to go it alone.

The days slipped by and, for a time, I walked with courage and with little concern toward my sickness. Things seemed to fall back in order as I attempted to push forward, proceeding with my life. The genital herpes had become somewhat manageable with medications and the syphilis I had been treated for and released. But the Hepatitis C, while still active in my body, had become silent and easily forgotten, with my personal belief that God would take care of it. Months later what I was determined to be healed from apparently became more determined than I to be known. I suddenly found myself tired and unable to keep motivated. I once again felt cold-like symptoms but mostly extreme fatigue. Slowly I begin to realize that something was severally wrong and once more on April 18, 2005, found myself in front of the Indian doctor. At the time of the appointment, I said very little other than my concerns. I agreed to further testing and once more attempted to share with him my beliefs that I would get through this with the Lord's help. That day, I left with hurt and confusion concerning my sickness and my faith in God. I once more found myself wondering why God was allowing this and if He really loved me. During this time, God had many ways of encouraging me. I repeatedly found myself in situations where I couldn't help but take notice of His presence and His peace. Many times during the night I was awakened and was lead to pray for others and sometimes even myself. I remember incredible dreams that often left me feeling hope and excitement, but more importantly, love for Him. Regardless of the experience one thing was constant... Each day I awoke to find my sickness ever present and my faith under steady attack.

The days after the appointment were a surprising improvement. It seemed that my fatigue was very quickly diminishing and my health seemed to be improving. By the end of the week I was back to my old self at work and was actually bouncing off the walls, unable to control all the excess energy. I couldn't explain it but I felt as though everything was different. Unexpectedly, I received a phone call at work one day. It was a nurse from my doctor's office. She began by telling me they had received my test results and would now need to set an appointment with another physician. She continued to inform me that because of my test results, the kidney specialist would no longer be able to help me. My case was now going to be transferred to an Infectious Disease Specialist. Immediately my mind raced, and I remember thinking I'm HIV positive. As I begin to question why I was being transferred; she, with confusion in her voice, begin to tell me that my test had come back clean. She attempted to reassure me that this did not mean I was healed but meant that someone with greater understanding and education would now have to review my test. I can't begin to express to you the excitement I felt as I hung up the phone. Almost in disbelief, what had seemed like a never ending curse had suddenly come to an end. Of course, I had another doctor's appointment but my faith that day was increased beyond measure.

On May 9, 2005, I once again found myself in the doctor's office being presented an opportunity to testify to the goodness of our Lord. With trembling hands and fear in my voice, I begin my story of how God had miraculously set me free from my past sexual confusion, drug addiction and even witchcraft. At the end of my testimony I received little to no recognition of my faith toward our Lord Jesus Christ. But I stood by faith and listened intently as this physician finally informed me that I had been spontaneously cured from Hepatitis C.

As of today I have been free from all signs and symptoms of Hepatitis C, and even Genitals Herpes since May 9, 2005. The Lord not only healed me of one but of **all** that mankind had promised me could never be cured. Today, I carry the medical reports from all three doctors in my brief case, seizing every opportunity to testify to the goodness and love our Lord.

* On April 02, 2007, I was, once again, tested for Hepatitis C, Genital Herpes, HIV, and Syphilis. The reports confirm and document that I am now negative on all accounts and have been medically released from future testing. (To God be all the Glory!)

In closing, I would like to leave you with several scriptures that not only stress the importance of our testimonies, but the power of our submission to God's will – even in fear and trembling. With every testimony given, we find greater victory in our lives, including but not limited to, our health and mental well being. Never forget that words have power and are only powerless when not spoken. Let me encourage each of you today, find someone and tell them of your victories in Christ. Exalt His name daily and live your life for Him because your freedom and well being came at a very high price.

Jesus speaking to the crowd:
"If anyone would come after me, he must deny himself and take up his cross and follow me. For whoever wants to save his life will lose it, but whoever loses his life for me and for the gospel will save it. What good is it for man to gain the whole world, yet forfeit his soul? OR what can a man give in exchange for his soul? If anyone is ashamed of me and my words in this adulterous and sinful generation, the Son of Man will be ashamed of him when he comes in his Father's glory with the holy angels."
Mark 8:34-38

That if you confess with your mouth, "Jesus is Lord," and believe in your heart that God raised him from the dead, you will be saved. For it is with your heart that you believe and are justified, and it is with your mouth that you confess and are saved. As the Scriptures says, "Anyone who trusts in him will never be put to shame."
Romans 10:9-11

Then I heard a loud voice in heaven say: Now have come the salvation and the power and the kingdom of our God, and the authority of His Christ. For the accuser of our brothers, who accuses them before our God day and night, has been hurled down. They overcame him by the blood of the Lamb and by the word of their testimony; they did not love their lives so much as to shrink from death.

REVELATION 12:10-11

To order additional copies of

From *Below* to *Above*

have your credit card ready and call
1 800-917-BOOK (2665)

or e-mail
orders@selahbooks.com

or order online at
www.selahbooks.com

To contact the Author for additional materials or to
schedule him as a guest speaker in your church or
area, please write or e-mail:

Below to Above Ministries
Shanahn Smith
P.O. Box 1604
Jasper, GA 30143
www.belowtoabove.com

Printed in the United States
202553BV00004B/172-267/P